APPROXIMATE DESIRE

The New Issues Press Poetry Series

The New Issues Press Poetry Series is sponsored by The College of Arts and Sciences, Western Michigan University, Kalamazoo, Michigan

An Inland Seas Poetry Book

Inland Seas poetry books are supported by a grant from The Michigan Council for Arts and Cultural Affairs.

First Edition, 1999.

ISBN: 0-932826-80-6 (paperbound)

Library of Congress Cataloging-in-Publication Data:
Thorburn, Russell
Approximate Desire / Russell Thorburn
Library of Congress Catalog Card Number (99-070685)

Art Direction :	Tricia Hennessy
Design:	Phil Foster
Production:	Paul Sizer The Design Center, Department of Art College of Fine Arts Western Michigan University
Printing:	Courier Corporation

APPROXIMATE DESIRE

RUSSELL THORBURN

New Issues Press

WESTERN MICHIGAN UNIVERSITY

For my three sons Gabriel, Christopher and Michael
For Rod Torreson

Contents

I

II

Acknowledgements

The author gratefully acknowledges the following magazines wherein many of these poems first appeared, sometimes in slightly different versions.

Aethlon: The Journal of Sport Literature: "Falling Through the Screen Again" and "Baseball Is a Metaphor."

Northeast: "Apollinaire's Hat," "Henry Zender Sees Ty Cobb in the Crowd at Belle Isle," and "Apollinaire Watches the White Sox Lose at Comiskey" (as "Apollinaire at a Baseball Game").

Parting Gifts: "Lesznianska Street Piano Lessons."

PrePress Awards: Volume Two: "Postcard from Montreal."

The Quarterly: "Apollinaire in America," "Apollinaire in the Midst of Bombardment," "The Company of Widows," "A Meditation on Loneliness in Minnesota," "The Day the Oaxaca Nine Played the Mexico City Kings," "After the Game," "The Right Fielder," and "Life on Lesznianska Street."

Third Coast: "After Einstein Walks out to View the Rooftops of Paris" (formerly "Einstein in Paris"), "Apollinaire Plays Catch with Ty Cobb," and "Tierra Blanca to Veracruz."

The author wishes to thank the National Endowment for the Arts, PEN/American, ArtServe, and the Michigan Council for the Arts and Cultural Affairs for their timely support during the writing of this book.

I describe Apollinaire's hat as a "drunken boat," which is a translation from the French of Rimbaud's "Le Bateau Ivre." I have borrowed a phrase from a Charles Simic poem for the same poem, "Apollinaire's Hat."

I would like to thank March Street Press for publishing two chapbooks of mine, a handful of those poems now appearing in this book; and to remember John Rybicki and Rod Torreson for their encouragement. I would like to thank Roberta Herter, Ron and Sheila Johnson and their son Jonathan, and Gordon Lish—and to bless the late, lively spirits of Phil Legler and John Woods.

I

Cocteau Painting a Mural of Angels in a Chapel in Villefranche while a Young Boy Holds His Ladder

Memory leaves a face
in the delicate wood chairs,
the Chinese slippers
placed under a coiffeuse.

What is given to me is the right
to draw a stillness that moves,
unlocking light and space.

I hang from the scaffolding.
An emptiness scolds us everywhere
for never choosing the heart.

What is there to fear
but the bitter promise of age,
the pungent, breathless flesh?

These walls pray
for a desperate flight.

Every sweet line reveals
more fullness until
each thigh or hip
would please a lover.

My assistant in silence
at the foot of the ladder watches
that stillness stare back
from the shoulders of angels.

Apollinaire in the Midst of Bombardment

Every explosion creates order.
I watch for what will happen next.
Mud flowers at the bottom of the trench,
and I see a garden in Montmartre, black stockings
brushing against roses, a woman's hand
opening to a face. I think of poetry,
how you start with a blank page.
Then a landscape crouches
around a shell's explosion.
I remember André Rouveyre's small coupe;
including his chauffeur, there were three of us,
and we said good-bye to an entire epoch,
driving from Deauville to Lisieux.

Another shell: look at the fan
of earth, the Frisian horses
with their sharp teeth.

Marie bit me back with each kiss,
the palms of her breasts
flattening against my chest.
How her armpits stared.

I gaze into a muddy mirror
and wonder why each glint of fire
erases my face.

The Physician Levi Looks upon the Wounded Apollinaire

When he arrives on a stretcher
pointing at his wound, I do not think
of healing him as much as catching
what he bleeds, that strong drink
from which men see visions.
I hear music suddenly so strange
his large head with its sloppy
bandage slips out of my hands.

Pulled inside out, I am weary
of not knowing answers to anything
but the way intestines are looped
back inside the stomach.

How much can I ask of the dead?
They gaze up at the doctor in his wire rims,
cleft chin, the funny little moustache
I promised to shave if I believed again.

"Doctor Levi, will I ever dance?"
He asks for a cigarette, this sad eyed Polack.
I light one for him. "Yes," I answer.
In trenches light fingers
the startled faces of soldiers.
"Doctor Levi," he says, lifting up from the stretcher.
There are no words for what's missing.

And the earth around us shudders from guns.
His hands brace him for falling,
his broad body and skinny legs: poetry
put together by such fear.

Shelled bodies in my spattered glasses:
the reconstruction of a leg,
or a head's broken enamel, every dizzying
aspect of the world waiting to be restored.

Apollinaire's Hat

His hat a drunken boat. Under it
he drowned in words.
Anybody who saw him on the Boulevard
first greeted his hat.

He hid the Eiffel Tower there.
Sometimes both of Picasso's hands
sketching the way a female body
becomes tragic architecture.

He was forced to spend nights writing
bad verse for money. His jailer
a hungry stomach. When he made love,
he wore the bowler.

That chamber where gods
advised him on women,
a pool in which he could hear
Time dripping.

How that hat grew in its own breath,
as if it were thinking along with him
about the body beneath it, waiting
for something to happen to change its life.

How it held the world in balance,
fit neatly over his head as it shaded
the view of the Luxembourg Gardens
and a whore with skinny legs.

His hat became an orator for his times;
if someone said hearts were made of stone,
he'd laugh, say his was pulled down tight
around his ears, melted like honey
upon his brow with its eternal smile.

Apollinaire Playing Tennis with Marie Laurencin

The ball sends him running in the back court,
a man with big shoulders and a sad face
who could be more Greek than French,
drawing both hands up on the racquet
as if to zing one into history
where her canvases show how abstract
flowers are, the apples and pears,
the men without still lives.
He cries out, sweating in his swing,
and knows there is nowhere else
to fall after her mother followed her
to his flat and waited outside his door,
seated on a large, braided mat.

And the ball lifts up into the air,
the poet not caring that a fragment
of *The Rite of Spring*
fills his head, and Marie swings
into the shadow of the ball
for a point, her long black skirt
pulled up in a victory dance.

"Dammit," he cries at her, "behave
like a woman," as she sticks out her tongue,
hands on her hips, flat-chested painter
with eyes much bigger than her face.
And he slaps the line where it went out,
calling her mistaken. But she saw it clearly,
and won't let him have the point.

"If you really need it," she says, "if you haven't
done enough with me in bed." Her knees
waking his memory of her, the speechless
shoulders leaning forward as he held
her small hips, the girl who brought her mother
with her to her lover's apartment. And the poet
learns what the men at Massada wondered, looking
down over the rocks, whether it was better
to jump or be captured by the Romans.
He walks around the net, still pointing,
knowing that pain never comes around right
until you name it.

After Einstein Walks out to View the Rooftops of Paris

The birds return to the balcony
where he calls a woman
three times from violent flight,
but his voice runs like water
over steps, and is gone. Her screaming begins,
and his young bride looks down
at the unexpected eddies of her shadow.

Her hair is streaming, each strand
passing blackness across her mouth.
He wants to find the place under her arm
where the skin is palest to kiss,
as if here were a woman's soul. As if
a soul could be mathematical,
pure and simple even in its sudden
complexity, like the stars that night
they lay on the divan pushed out
onto the balcony. Hysterical, she drops
her black silk dress from the railing.

She has smashed the wedding cake;
he turns away, unable to comfort her,
and glimpses the eternal,
not a religious panel
but melancholy numbers.

Oh to sit with God in a lawn chair,
but he'd settle for this:
to have her stop screaming,
for theories on light and its speed
have left her crazy, weeping at his feet.

Apollinaire Listens to Einstein Talk about Relativity

We're floating in circles
on the Seine, almost colliding
with a punt, so many circles,
I have to tell him to stop
rowing so I can take the oars:
that's when the fire of his mathematics
lights his eyes, his shirt unbuttoned
to the chest, and he tells me
about the way the world will end.
How it's like catching fireflies,
little photons cupped in a hand
that release their light, grow graceful
in their quickness until they die.

His straw hat clawed
off in a glance at the blue sky,
he notes every dot toward
infinity, every point
brushed into a whole,
while our craft cuts the water.

The blue in the rippling Seine
flickers onto a canvas
we have become a part of, the mathematician
standing in the boat with its bow
bent into the waves, looking for the way
the future will flow, his large hat doffed
in tribute to a gull, its gliding
eternally precise as if it could last
long after eyes glance away
from the colors the Comedian daubed
without thinking what would follow.

Apollinaire in America

This bus courses over the bones of America.
The wisdom of each prairie
rolled up into tumbleweed
about to blow away.

One riverbed is flooded with light.
Somewhere north of here,
in the great cathedral of dust,
horses gallop; you weep
without knowing why.

Einstein Married to Mileva

Last night her disingenuous face told him
their wedding was a mistake.
Still, love was catlike and could land
on its feet, or whisper sweet words
to the sunlight on the boulevard
where a woman with bare legs drove
the horse-drawn cart.

He had suggested an hour
on the Seine, rowing. She dressed
for a hurricane, thick stockings and a hat
that weeps all over her face: the boat rented
to row out to that middle place
where he could release
the oars to drift back toward desire.

Her sunhat like so many flowers
tossed from her lap, diverted
to a water so blue she'd gladly
die there, content to gaze up
at an aging sky never cracked enough
to be pieced together whole.

So far she can see only what the weather offers,
how the clouds twist their scaffolding
into place; but the landed boat jars
her back to the world, her hands lifting
the thin, black dress up around her legs.

How much of everything is torn already,
even this private slipstream
as she juggles her windblown hair
and whispers at the soft-shouldered Albert
waiting in the water, his trousers
rolled up to the knees, her husband
with his mad hair, the oars outstretched
above his head, a Greek hero
home from the sea.

This Is How Every Century Begins

How the world can be destroyed
is an unbelievable dream,
a fire feeding on beauty.

While a fresh cigar is lit
by an Ukrainian waitress,
Einstein's smile wakens

the unified field of his desire,
his napkin wiping away the bad love
of his Serbian wife, the stained linen

stripped by the Ukrainian beckoning
behind silk. Her tight brown smock
with its own ordered parts.

If he could only find the precise point
love ended another could begin
in this outdoor café

under linden trees,
where every flaw in a woman is part
of the equation.

Cocteau in the Village of Milly-la-Forêt, Near Fontainebleau

The best day's work
was when you sat down
in an Adirondack chair,
the brilliant white of a pad
propped against your knees,
and sketched nothing,
letting the shadow of your hands
move in slow
pantomime across paper.

The absence of everything
was refreshing, and you could not leave,
as you pretended to pour
the mysteries of color
onto that canvas by wiggling
your fingers, giving them mouths,
sometimes tails, like wolves

if anyone might have asked, wolves
who preyed upon
those Sumerian voids where
anything Biblical pulsed like pain,
and anything else grew dark
with revelation.

Taking off your socks, you admired
your toes,
saw the blue veins
like the subtle work of time, each foot
brought down from the mountains.

II

Life on Lesznianska Street

Everything we are is in this canvas,
or what remains, the body,
its fibers plucked from a golden nap
bristling with the subtle reminder:
each of us is invisible to the other.

The evening knots with light.
I am alive like a mirror,
the paint struggling
to assemble my thoughts.

When he is not aware of it,
I watch for what he admits.

Death marks our lives; we count
on it to turn the calendar.
If not from hunger, then from random shootings.
"Finished?" he asks.

We are bodies.
What bullet will pin us to earth?
The point of this work. The assemblage.

Two Variations on a Painting by Matisse

(after Piano Lesson, *his son practicing*
before the mobilization of Paris, 1916)

I

While his friends
belly up to the green-shuttered windows
to admire breathtaking leaps
his fingers take in each octave,
the metronome steals his afternoon
from Chinese hairs on slender-tipped brushes.

The pianist hasn't breathed
in several octaves, his left hand ambling
among flowers while his right
launches an assault up the scales
in his teacher's notebook
where the master scrawled *silence*
as a way of beating noise to its drums.

II

Every chord arches his small hands
before they collapse into music.
He falls through the floor
of so many notes
he won't ever be able to walk
into Chopin again.

If he could get inside the piano
and float downstream on each crescendo.
But he drowns most of the time
in too many notes,
his headache asking his father
if he could stop to rest
on the damp summer shore
of the blue couch.

Lesznianska Street Piano Lessons

My piano teacher
holds his hands
so still, it is the rest
of the world trembling.

Postcard from Montreal

The picture shows the botanic garden,
how she must have left it, sunny
and menacing; the other side
a breath away, when she found in her regrets
a language ripe as grapes
to fit into the smallest space.

But you read the postcard,
turning it around to note the words
scribbled-in edgewise
from a pencil that has long been
overdue for a sharpening.
Each impression is soft as she:
plump bare legs
and long brown hair tailing
her back in a pony.

You find what she is trying
to say only later, after wine,
walking the sweet-winded streets
of the September night,

adrift with your thoughts,
thinking how long she has been away,
when she will come back
and what you will do together.

And then this persistent desire,
which is portable, and fits onto a postcard,
is slipped out of your pocket,
and you read it again.

He Drank the Sun Down Ashamed of the Way We Treated Her

Where did he find her and did he take
comfort in women our age, letting her sleep
in our house? Our cursing over her
another language we cupped to our mouths.

How his impractical spleen made us
see more clearly her dark brown hair,
her face still staring into ripples
an oar left, as if deep down she were being tugged.
But we could not help ourselves, and insulted
her more, taking stock of her varicose veins
when she slid her jeans off to a single-piece suit.

We were convinced she was a mermaid
who let him breathe
through her mouth underwater before
spoiling the surface where frogs reposed
on lily pads like royalty—and not
a middle-aged accountant Father dated
after Mother died in the cancer ward.

Mother seeing through us
while we watched the mermaid
in her one-piece, wondering how she flipped
her tail out from those human feet,
her armpits full of black hair,
her double chin our specialty
for each foulmouthed curse
we cast into space.

Black flies huddled while Father licked
her ears and the day seemed to stop
out on the delicate bone of a lake.
When we ached from pulling his weight
back from the water, his eyes
large as knuckles and his gray hair slicked
over that barrel of a chest,
we heard Mother say, "Let him love
what dragged him down."

The Company of Widows

These pigeons she brushes aside
without a word.
If she did speak,
she would tell them
about garlic
in her underwear drawer.

She would march across
the snowy roof
to the ache of her room
and point to her sleeping husband
beneath the begonias.

Her furniture
sinks into the snow.

A scarf fluttering against a cheek,
she stands pearled with pigeons
and waits for a savage to dance
on the street, someone
to summon her from sleep.

Saint-Germain-des-Prés

The poet is arrested sooner or later, shoved
roughly into a dark cell where he hangs himself
with his own poems. When he is brought down
and laid out on the floor, the ceremony of praise
awakens him. He glimpses the deep blue sky
of a woman's eyes. "If you never write another
poem, don't worry," her voice bathes the forehead
of the hanged man. He never sleeps longer
than he has to after that. He is taken to Saint-
Germain-des-Prés to sit for a half hour,
feel the pulse wire up his heart, and listen
to Latin clean out his arteries.
An epicurean palate is awakened at a café
where the first sip of coffee confirms the Ascension
of Christ and the soup sans any regrets
jiggles in a small bowl, the baguettes
broken like the backs of martyrs, buttered
at the last moment to ease the pain
of an empty belly.

The Eiffel Tower

You have your own Eiffel Tower,
a way of looking at the world
afraid the latest poem to take language

into the Chinese or French has been written
by someone else. And you look at the newspapers,
understanding you are not again in the news,

have not won any prizes that the journalists
may or may not have reported, and let failure
smart against your cheeks, the mind blow out

the same old gods sleeping in foreign ports.
And if what you've written can't satisfy
even the lowest circle of Hell's critics,

then damn them, and move on.
Your fucking Eiffel Tower is portable,
and if you want pigeons to swirl

above your head, they're welcome.
You can be happy where ants crawl
over old vanishing roads and fires burn

in women who sweep clean their doorways
of white granules; where handmade carts
bear the burden of morning;

and you know any day
you can jump from yourself into another body
as easily as your forsaken soul

rises from flesh undone and quivering
while dogs sniff the fundamental question:
who will inherit your house

where you have paid out rent
for the Eiffel Tower in your head?

The Seine

Let's try locating the cattails
further downriver, or submerged fish
who are writing their own poems
about beauty.

If not fish, let's look at the perspective
of a frog on a lily pad, one of those
dreamlike half-white, half-pink
pads the waves rock.

Or the color of the water itself,
the off-blue, almost grey-blue surface
that reflects the cold sky
washed clean by clouds.

Every day sadness teaches us
to measure the good in people,
so that in a poem leaking across the river
we breathe the melancholy.

And for the longest moment
we are pulled toward the center of something
we don't believe in, wondering
what has happened to the color.

Not at all like the one we began with,
but who's there to instruct us
where we've gone wrong?
The oars lifted from the water.

Hotel Eros

In a hotel whose name
we don't remember, your blue robe,
unfathomable in its sashed knot, unties:

the Book of Imponderable Gestures
opens to Eros. Your three-year-old
daughter plays with water at the sink.

We are turning pages past desire,
pausing at erogenous, your eyelids
blinking, as if remembering agape.

The child, our blonde-haired Cupid.
A roomful of erotic tricks. What is love
but a chair with a hard back

creaking us past aeromancy and synapse,
our own forecast for sexual weather?
The daughter glances at the man

who has loved her like a father,
the mother who rises, finally,
her brown hair loosened to her waist,

to slide the curtains aside. Sunrise, and time
for the gods to crowd this moment
with all we have discovered of loss.

A Meditation on Loneliness in Minnesota

A hand in a Buick miles away
releases your letters
back to the blackness.

A late-night TV show burns
the room, where Gideon's Bible
lies fat with judgment.

Bitch, you cry to this flown bird
who uses your credit card
to track the prairie
and nest in a shadowy bed,
who wears satin
and dances with a stranger
who slips his hands under her blouse.

What good are words anymore?
The wind steals your cry,
your wife. In the deep fields,
her accomplice,
your eyes search the wind
for her hair.

She becomes the actress
pleading with Tyrone Power.

This B movie
runs day and night;
you bow your head.
The evening flickers through your palms.

Film Noir

If they were coming after me and death
was certain, would I think of you,
our suburban drive through the snow?
They wouldn't have to promise pain
for me to remember the poor were never
the right ones to die, or for me
to see clearly those streets
we drove one night, the snow-burdened
houses, the snow itself withholding judgment
on a man and a woman turning the corner
of the same neighborhood over and over.
I could feel the tires keeping
to the road while we slid
and I blessed every one of my persecutors,
real or imaginary, who knew the value
of eliminating all witnesses
from scenes that could never be forgiven;
and our own scenario: a couple
who never thought of parting.
Where were the witnesses who could say
he screamed to the end?
A snowy night seemed to give the world
boundaries, your name
spoken while a wealth of cold made
us shiver. Time allowed us
to smile upon houses embarrassed
by so many strung lights.
Your family came from Holland,
and you told me how to swerve
the steering wheel back so we would inscribe a circle
on the frozen dark.

You laughed as we spun about,
and I knew some day I would shout
that pain of never hearing your voice again,
nor lying down beside you, my last minutes
come with your name on my lips,
the snow still falling.

III

The Day the Oaxaca Nine Played the Mexico City Kings

Near sunset a pink light catches fire. He whispers to his
hands,
"I am nobody," and walks out to right field, his heavy
mitt weeping
for the ball. He remembers the men at work on the
irrigation project,
the thirteen who formed the Oaxaca Nine. They were
supposed to wear bright
uniforms that announced Dow to the spectators. But
some of them proposed that
they would be on the field and not Dow. They wore the
shirts inside out.
A batter swings at a pitch: a dialogue between air and
catcher's mitt.
He dreams of his wife's face, the noble brown features
that seem
to be part of the sunset, the growing shadows. He sees
the lie on her
face when he asks if the pain is more or less today. But
what can he do,
he who makes so little by working so hard?
The next swing is one of fire, the bat's wood baptizing
the ball.
He sees it but does not see it at the same time.
The ball skids across the grass.
Six children he would mourn that day.
He pounds his hot mitt and dreams
the ball is a prehistoric egg.
"All of us who die leave broken things behind," he
cries. He stares
up into the pink fire, ashamed of catches he never
made, a bat that was
blind in stroking a ball past his knowing.

The Right Fielder

Drawing close to the billboard, he loses the ball to the
 lights.
He lifts his mitt, guessing at the ball that pours across
 leather and streams
through the hands of a disbelieving fan. The dust
 does not give up his shame,
nor his wife's suffering in the seats. Walking
 back to the dugout,
he listens to voices that chastise.
"Rodriguez," the short manager breathes, the one
who would always be knuckling in his life now,
who got him the job working for Dow.
His name is a withered flower.
He hears the fans who lose their voices again
 in the ninth, sees the clear water
of the moon out early in its judgment.
He turns, his few remaining pesos disappear into
 the neighborhood.
He peers into the manager's face that knows
 where he is going and what
he will be doing, what he will look like in the morning,
 and asks himself if ever
there will be a day without this knowledge.

Tierra Blanca to Veracruz

He gazes dreamily at the soldier with the rifle,
knows the dead tree across the road
is for an ambush, the bus slowing down,
as he closes his eyes, remembers how Nijinsky
danced in Mexico City, and he sat
next to Blaise Cendrars and Leon Trotsky.

This joy he has never revealed to anyone
but his wife, who told him: "You expect me
to sleep with a ballet-lover?" His reply:
"Your heart can never match this ruined mitt."

The rainforest rattling in the rain,
he wipes sweat from his eyes: Ramirez
who lost second place for the Oaxaca Nine
with his bad-hearted glove
in right field, who hummed Stravinsky's score
when he wandered into the dugout,
after the night of the opera.

With a hand against his right breast
he shouts down to the rebels who have bloomed.
"Let me be the first bastard shot,
pledge this honor in a bullet to me."

Their cheers bitter as the brown water
they drink in this region, they motion
with their machetes for the bus to pass,
but not until they have stripped a junk-balling left-hander,
whom they promptly address with their only gun and shoot.

After the Game

He kicks at the dirt, raising cigarette butts and candy
wrappers at home plate. They drove all night from
Oaxaca to lose to the Mexico City Kings, and he
sees the long way back to that crowd in Oaxaca,
will find the grave already dug for his mitt. So he
dreams of his body exploding against the billboard,
the ball dropping before him on the grass, the
runners moving around the basepaths, their legs
striving for the wheat-colored plate. He lifts up an
arm, as if at the last minute he could catch something
other than a janitor mocking him with his broom.

Baseball Shoes Found in the Jungle by Lieutenant Carreno

The cleats grin fiercely
back at fate as if no matter
how hard one stares
one can never vanish
into happiness. Each tooth
beaded with dirt from games
the world has already swallowed.

Each shoe with a face
that gathered dirt from a game
insignificant as the rain,
or the hunger in the lieutenant's stomach,
or the man who was killed and forgotten.
Now his cleats are the only
important lesson, the teeth
that grip terra firma
as the lieutenant fills his elephantine
pocket with lost games, looking
at where the soldiers have dug a place
in the red-wet clay for a junk-baller
who threw left-handed, his mitt
fit onto a swollen hand, the other horn
curled and missing two fingers
and a thumb.

They empty his bag, scatter
letters back to their original inspiration:
the wind. Letters can be found in the trees,
foolish letters to an even more foolish whore
named Juanita, who will not remember him
when they collect these fictions
and tie them with a garter and set them out
among her rotted squash, each in its own way
telling her how the earth is hers.

Henry Zender Sees Ty Cobb in the Crowd at Belle Isle

I'm forty-three, my first wife
dead for five years;
when I sit too long in the sunlight,
I remember my other wife,
her body an iceberg, her voice
a cross-cut saw chewing up my daughters.

If I can't drink beer in the sunshine
and listen to Italian singers frighten
birds from the elms, damn both
of them. I look into the crowd
for what I don't know, unless it's
a feeling of vertigo when a woman
unties her mouth's pink bow.

Outdoors, beer always tastes better,
but when so many parasols spin above
the heads of women, the whole picture
is lost to the curl of a yellow
hat feather, high breasts grasped
by corset bone, a head turning.

That's when I stand up from my chair
and find, dammit, Ty Cobb
in the arrogance of a simple white shirt
snugly buttoned,
as if its pinching reminds him of his day off
from the wars at Navin Field.

That son of a bitch, his own beer in hand,
gazing at women, waiting for an eye-twitch,
the ache of a bosom, as if ready
to steal past the stiff chairs.

For a second, our eyes meet the same dark
in miles and miles of days broken by hard work.

Drunk, you look for what you've lost,
hoping to get it back; underneath a cloud,
Ty Cobb waves to you with the grace of a god.

Apollinaire Plays Catch with Ty Cobb

In the heat of July at Navin Field
    where he watched
the Tigers beat the White Sox, he spits
    into his mitt,
rubs a place where Cobb's throw would
    ache,
then promptly winces after that son of a bitch
    pegs one at his neck.
He hears the seams in the baseball
    talk about death,
the pill bobbled in his hand, as the Georgia Peach
calls out, "Parlez-vous that one, Fatboy,"
    the fortune of twenty bucks
thick in his pocket: the bill for a simple game of catch.
But stilling the life of the ball, the poet
    looks at his own death
he saw back in the trenches, the signature it left
    in his head,
and challenges the King of Spikes: "Throw me one
where I will see both the past and the present
    in the spinning seams,
knuckle one against the grain of the new moon."

The Detroit outfielder in his pinstriped suit
    and a bowler
eyes the ball that slowly returns through the same
    air it had traveled,
catches it as if looking into his own father's death,
    and grips the ball
until there is no breath left in it and the air
    is to be pitied
as well as the poet. And Cobb laughs twice
    before windmilling

a rock into a dense blue of night, yelling out,
    "Here comes that moon, fella,
better catch it," the ball rising until its death
    can be clearly seen.

Apollinaire exchanges greetings with both the moon
    and the ball:
"Here I am prepared to die under two gods, baseball
    and poetry."
The ball tearing off his mitt and Cobb walking away,
    singing a tune
to twenty bucks. Everywhere black on the field.

The Art of the Fastball

Their fists knuckled on wood,
swinging at what they could not stop,
some mystery like Homer's.

Their cracking voices showing
their bodies were going through a change
as they walked back to the dugout
after flailing at fastballs
flung with guile, fingers overlapping
the stitches that were like scars
from Greek wars.

How I rubbed my curse into cowhide
about to see them swing at air,
wondering how poetry
made me throw faster
than other thirteen year olds,
why I drew in Zeus

and his mansions, human places
where a body could wander,
like Cyprus or Phoenicia,
as if knowing that their strangeness

gave me power that busted
in on them, an incantation
hot as those pastures, where their best
was to foul off pitches.

When I was thirteen Greek myths
were terrible as an older sister's body
in a bathing suit, the engine
a father dropped into an old car.

I threw until all magic wore off
from the stitches and each ball grip
with its time-worn prophecy
echoed in the catcher's cave
where the rattling chicken bones
of some oracle pronounced each man
mortal and bound to fall.

Apollinaire Watches the White Sox Lose at Comiskey

Ty Cobb rounds the bases, the crowd
shouting for the ball to cut
this son of a bitch off at the knees.

The waitress' legs are there, too,
a woman with dark red hair
who bore coffee to you at a diner,

as Cobb's home plate slide
draws blood when the catcher bends
with the ball. How you piece
together all these fragments:

a woman's long legs,
the night you rode to Lisieux
in André Rouveyre's coupe,
the catcher crumpling in pain

as the umpire signals safe,
and everyone knows he's out,
the crowd spewing peanuts,
beer, and apples,

and you rise with the recovered Cobb,
knowing something about legs,
the simple beauty in the calves
where the blue stockings are attached.

The catcher dances around the umpire
stoic in black as Cobb
walks away, a part of the eternal,
and you stand there with them, shouting
at your own gods of poetry.

Baseball Is a Metaphor

is what you are thinking
when you stand beside the diamond
after your son's game and everyone has vanished,
and you kick the plate,
the candy wrappers, the cigarettes.

At best, you are an average man
who has made nothing of himself, conducted
yourself as if you were always meant
to watch your son's game as a stranger,
ducking your head whenever he looked
for the wheat-chaff of praise, anything
cut up or mown, milkweed, ragweed,
he didn't care how beautiful the words.

Each time he bats, twelve years old
and as shy as you are, he swings from vertigo,
you kicking him as well
as yourself to reach the high, tight pitches
you were afraid to address
in the game's milk white tension.

You kick him even
on the bench, head down
like you—that's your try
at grasping truth or metaphor—
if you kept your head in, you could
drive it hard up the country.

When you pull off the ball, that's when
you cut through the air, work the words
into their own dark corridors,
feel their teeth. There will always be
strikeouts, their presence around you
like an angry manager demanding blood.

Falling Through the Screen Again

It takes days to get there, behind home plate,
the other side of fatherhood.
I'm straining with this engine,
my heart, over each hill,
to find you there.

Christopher, we will flick on our mitts,
put a fire into our game,
hoping that who we are
will sizzle into the other's pocket.

You will swim grass,
the sky blossoming around you,
sip air
as if it were milk.

Poetry begins with a ball,
then a bat, this sudden baptism
by wood, and the fly ball
shimmering, your hanging
onto the bead, working
the air deep, until
you fall into the catch.

Apology to My Father

I wear this faded brown mitt,
snap one back to my son
in this dialogue of fastballs,
this brilliant blue sky
losing something more than what
is gained, as I remember telling
my father I hated baseball,
who threw a lob that held angels up
as it shadowed me, the catcher,
waiting for his sad face
to fall: "Look, I have made mistakes."

I set my arm
and become the eternal son,
all stone and ancient,
who zips one into the calm smell
of spring, hearing his own father
like so many zither strings
pluck the melody from the air.
His eyes become patient,
looking back into my eyes
as if it didn't matter
how much we broke each other's heart.

The Photograph

Who knows when flesh folds
under, when wrinkles appear
where there was only youth?

Those mirrors we slide out of drawers
hold us shimmering.

Faraway places scribbled
on the back in pencil, the once sharp
point of departure

now blurred but readable.
Tachov, Bohemia
on the baptismal certificate.

A great-grandmother who lived
at 90 Purschau, with the name
of Roschenthaler.

Rilke and My Great-Aunts and Grandmother

The trolley conductor asks, "What was wrong
with him? He just stood there, as if listening
to something." The children shake their heads,
thinking of themselves already,
the stepmother who will steal the tavern,
their father in the arms of the conductor
who carries him back to the sanctuary of grass
he has left to walk across the road.
My great-aunts and grandmother as teenagers
flap there in swelling skirts, on that
1912 summer afternoon at Belle Isle, with
their French faces, the bobbed hair of youth.
They think about how to begin again.

None of them would think of Rilke as an answer,
the German poet who wrote about a man
who had lost his wife to death,
that season of parties and slow dances.
They would not have known about Eurydice,
who didn't want to be rescued,
nor feel the irony that they had lost their father
while their cruel stepmother lived.

From the Tuileries to a chateau in the sexual
Alps, the Zender girls would never have known
about Rilke's tragedies, nor cared
about the words of a poem, with their own dark
implications: "His senses felt as though
they were split in two," which I am reading now
for my great-aunts, for my great-grandfather, Henry,
who knew only that he had stood in a road,
unsure if death could be like this, thinking
about his first wife, never knowing his great-grandson

would hold one of Rilke's poems in his hand, and read it
slowly, wondering who can belong to whom, once dead,
the words ripening in his thorax, unsure of his own life,
at forty-five.

Rainer and Clara

The light itself breaks open
as if we have never known nakedness.
So the night spills out its
plaster-casts of panthers
and words that are always departing,

or hands that have made memory
into a kind of art, without ever touching.
We are strangers
and *nothing* is a hand shaping things,
a hand needing no arm to bring
into motion the stillness of the heart.

Marie Zender

If she could talk, she'd tell you
how you got her father all wrong
in your poem, how he was
already dead as he drank
the hours blue in his saloon,
how her father, Henry, saw his three
daughters as Degas-like,
with their French looks
ready to be pinned up on the wall
of somebody's desire, how his eyes
pinned other women with full thighs
and bare white throats who
sidestepped strangers, her own father
drinking to the wide boulevards
of Detroit, the iron gates of parks
swung open, inviting pleasure
to be sweet as water cupped
in thirsty hands. She would whisper
how beer entered his heart,
this Swiss immigrant and president
of the Detroit Swiss Club,
who marched its members
through his saloon doors
every Thursday and never let them go,
who walked into the streetcar
at Belle Isle, drunk on himself,
that August day in 1912,
eaten by his own sweat, looking
back at his daughters, his last glance
like a torch against her cheek.

Henry Zender Sees His Wife in a Coffin

All day I've waited to see her hands folded,
a mouth not right telling me,
"Henry, don't be so hard on the girls,
marry someone with a good heart
once I'm gone."

She lies there expecting
a kiss from a stranger
who has wrung every offered hand,
our waltz into love forgotten.

That's me with the white rose in my lapel,
the eyes like stiff drinks, all in black,
and a chafing white shirt, a stud
piercing shut the collar.

Three daughters bolster me with their good looks,
the fancy smell of grief perspiring from
under their chins and arms, their whispers
like roses brushing against the watermark
of Dutch paper: "Papa, don't drink too much."

I push toward the coffin with a murmuring
heart, dive toward her mouth,
my head almost falling into the blue silk;
my hands grasping hers blossom
into a deeper bouquet.

"Forgive me" was what I'd say for ignoring her,
drinking every night until there was
only morning left. Then rising fat
and forgetful in my clothes.

The kiss meets her mouth, but my cheek
sticks to the paste of the dead,
the rouge with its burnt-out sunsets,
when I pull away to look upon Anna.

Her thin face caught in the act of something
that would never come, the high, ripe cheeks
discerning, dead with three daughters.
I would say it for her: "You were never
good enough for me."

The Living Who Are Wearing My Clothes

don't even say hello on the street, walk right
by me as if I were someone else
who has combed his hair in a new, exciting way.
I don't think of myself as dead, but I close my eyes
so whole new rivers and mountains appear
where there are none. Sometimes the Eiffel Tower
is lying on its side, or I go to places where I have never sat
for the sunset, and drop my head in shame
for ever doubting beauty in the world could make
rivers run backwards, cigarette smoke turn purple,
a tenth cup of coffee taste like Dom Pérignon,
or Sacré-Coeur reveal the heart of Christ
during Holy Week. When I wear death
I walk more strangely than I should, mumbling
the shirt's too loose, or the trousers won't stay up,
I've lost so much weight.

Hotel Memory

What one remembers
is its own machine
where genesis begins in grief.

Let a glass of water
address the late hour

as one trembles
at the face of a clock.

Chairs, slid out,
hint at conversations

like cracked cups,
the fridge leaking its winter.

The double business of words
educates the ear

as the dark pulls through the magnet
of a window our own staring faces.

What we do with each other
is bound in the eye

the late hours searching
for what we could have possibly been.

photo by Emily Thorburn

Russell Thorburn was born in Birmingham, Michigan. Such journals as *Third Coast*, *Aethlon: The Journal of Sport Literature*, and *The Quarterly* have published his work. He has been awarded grants from the National Endowment for the Arts, the Michigan Council for Arts and Cultural Affairs, ArtServe, and PEN/American. He has taught poetry to prison inmates, and worked with emotionally impaired students. He currently lives in Marquette, Michigan, where he's raising three sons.

New Issues Press Poetry Series

James Armstrong, *Monument in a Summer Hat*

Anthony Butts, *Fifth Season*

Gladys Cardiff, *A Bare Unpainted Table*

Lisa Fishman, *The Deep Heart's Core Is a Suitcase*

Lance Larsen, *Erasable Walls*

David Dodd Lee, *Downsides of Fish Culture*

Deanne Lundin, *The Ginseng Hunter's Notebook*

David Marlatt, *A Hog Slaughtering Woman*

Paula McLain, *Less of Her*

Malena Mörling, *Ocean Avenue*

Julie Moulds, *The Woman With a Cubed Head*

Marsha de la O, *Black Hope*

Rebecca Reynolds, *Daughter of the Hangnail*

John Rybicki, *Traveling at High Speeds*

Diane Seuss-Brakeman, *It Blows You Hollow*

Marc Sheehan, *Greatest Hits*

Angela Sorby, *Distance Learning*

Russell Thorburn, *Approximate Desire*

Patricia Jabbeh Wesley, *Before the Palm Could Bloom: Poems of Africa*